Fables & Folktales

Raven the Trickster

by Tyler Gieseke

Dash!
LEVELED READERS
An Imprint of Abdo Zoom • abdobooks.com

Level 1 – Beginning
Short and simple sentences with familiar words or patterns for children who are beginning to understand how letters and sounds go together.

Level 2 – Emerging
Longer words and sentences with more complex language patterns for readers who are practicing common words and letter sounds.

Level 3 – Transitional
More developed language and vocabulary for readers who are becoming more independent.

abdobooks.com

Published by Abdo Zoom, a division of ABDO, PO Box 398166, Minneapolis, Minnesota 55439.

Printed in the United States of America, North Mankato, Minnesota.
102025
012026

Photo Credits: ABDO, Adobe Stock, Getty Images, Shutterstock
Production Contributors: Jennie Forsberg, Grace Hansen, Tyler Gieseke
Design Contributors: Candice Keimig, Neil Klinepier, Colleen McLaren

Library of Congress Control Number: 2025936789

Publisher's Cataloging in Publication Data

Names: Gieseke, Tyler, author.
Title: Raven the trickster / by Tyler Gieseke
Description: Minneapolis, Minnesota : Abdo Zoom, 2026 | Series: Fables & folktales | Includes online resources and index.
Identifiers: ISBN 9798384940067 (lib. bdg.) | ISBN 9798384940821 (ebook) | ISBN 9798384941200 (read-to-me ebook)
Subjects: LCSH: Ravens--Juvenile literature. | Indians of North America--Folklore--Juvenile literature. | Tricksters--Juvenile literature. | Folk literature, American--Juvenile literature. | Cultural identity--Juvenile literature. | Intellect of animals--Juvenile literature. | Folktales--Juvenile literature.
Classification: DDC 398.2 [E]--dc23

Table of Contents

Fables & Folktales 4

Raven the Trickster 6

Lessons 14

More Facts 22

Glossary 23

Index 24

Online Resources 24

Fables & Folktales

Fables and folktales are both kinds of stories. Fables are usually short. They teach a clear **lesson**. They often include talking animals.

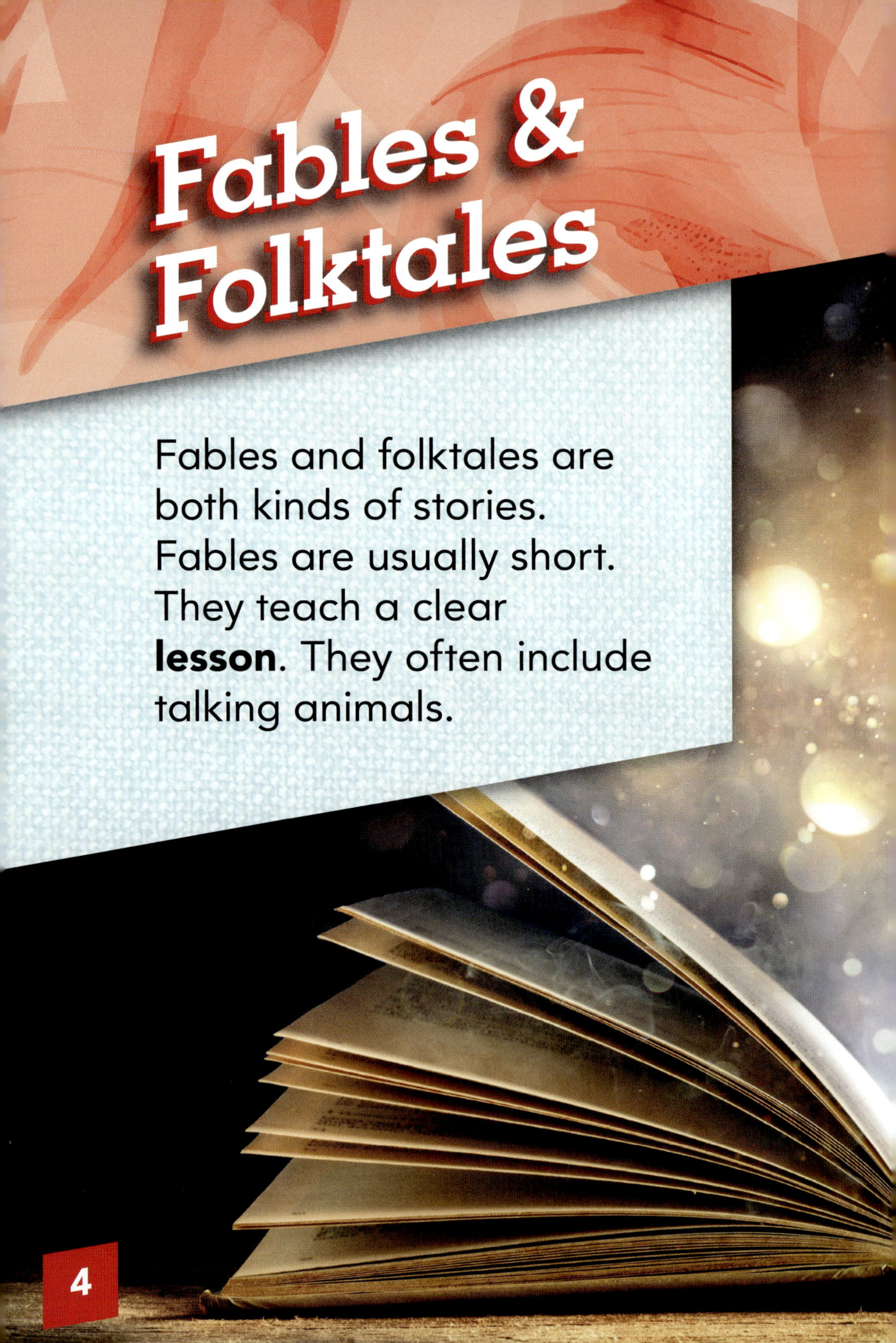

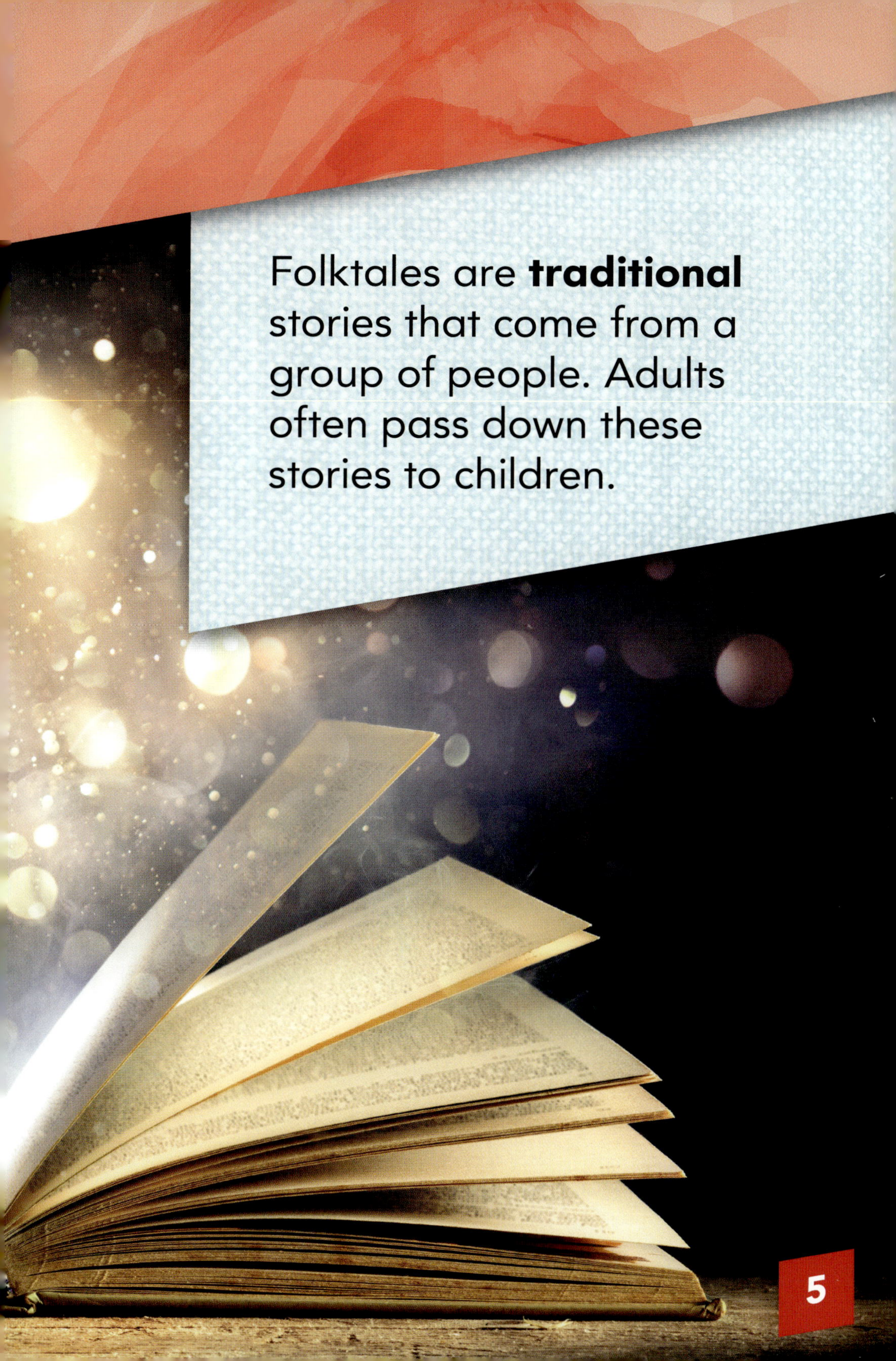

Folktales are **traditional** stories that come from a group of people. Adults often pass down these stories to children.

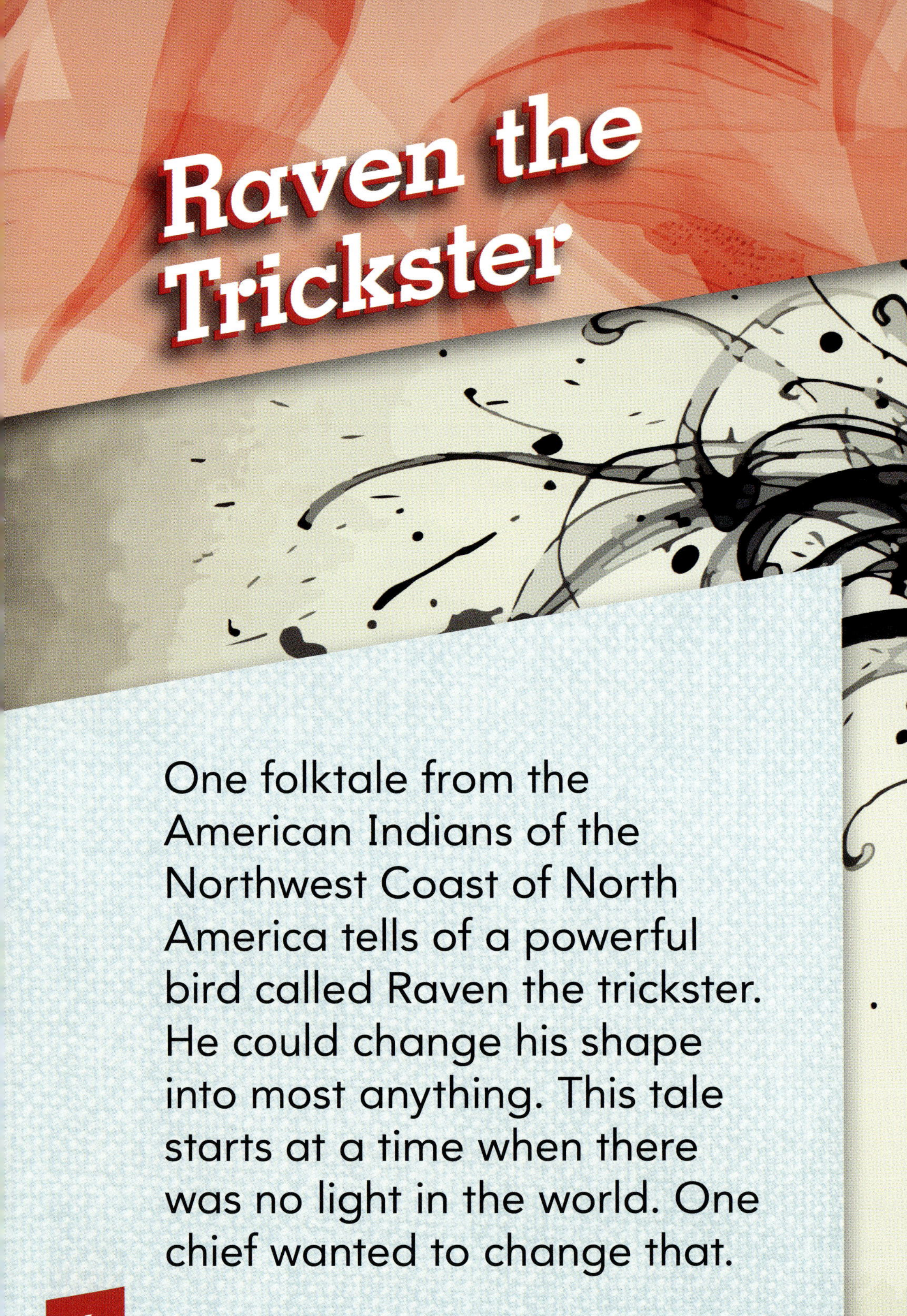

Raven the Trickster

One folktale from the American Indians of the Northwest Coast of North America tells of a powerful bird called Raven the trickster. He could change his shape into most anything. This tale starts at a time when there was no light in the world. One chief wanted to change that.

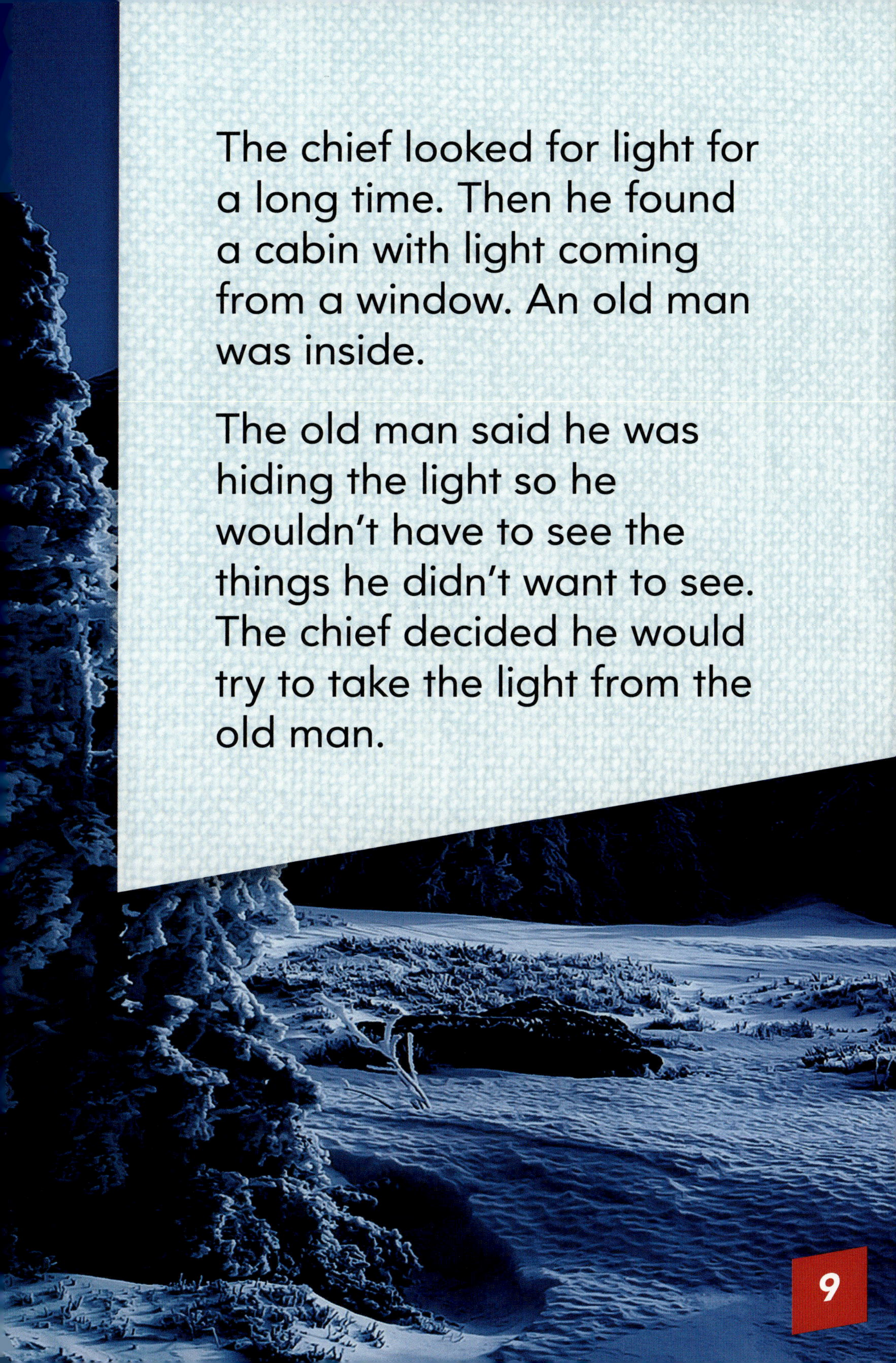

The chief looked for light for a long time. Then he found a cabin with light coming from a window. An old man was inside.

The old man said he was hiding the light so he wouldn't have to see the things he didn't want to see. The chief decided he would try to take the light from the old man.

First, the chief and his villagers tried to reason with the old man. They told him that things he didn't like existed even if he couldn't see them. But the old man still wouldn't give up the light. Then the chief and his villagers tried to break open the box where the light was kept.

But only the old man knew the code to open the box. Finally, the chief asked Raven to help.

Raven **transformed** into a small boy. The old man had always wanted a grandson, so he invited him in. When the boy asked to see the light, the old man agreed to show him.

As soon as the box was open, Raven turned back into a bird and knocked the box to the ground. The sun, moon, and stars escaped from the box! This is why the world has light.

Lessons

A folktale often goes beyond the story itself to teach powerful **lessons**. One lesson from the tale of Raven the trickster is that you can't **avoid** the things you don't like in the world. The old man tries to pretend the things he doesn't like don't exist. This keeps the light from everyone.

But the truth is we must **admit** to the things we don't like in the world. For example, you might not get along with some people in your class. But you can't pretend they don't exist.

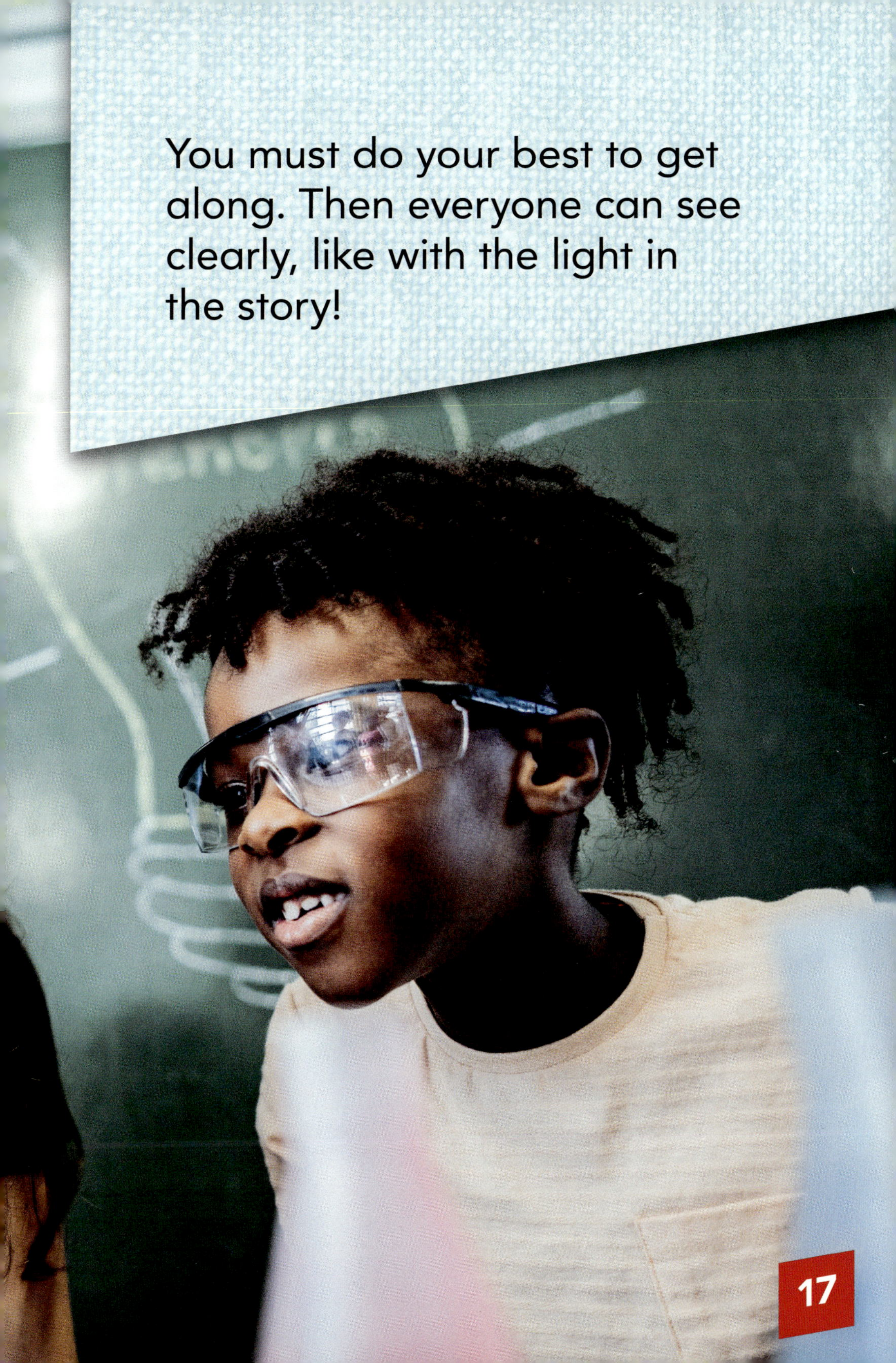

You must do your best to get along. Then everyone can see clearly, like with the light in the story!

Another **lesson** from this folktale is that the natural world offers many things people need. In the story, the chief and the villagers can't get the light on their own. They must **rely** on the help of the powerful animal Raven to help them.

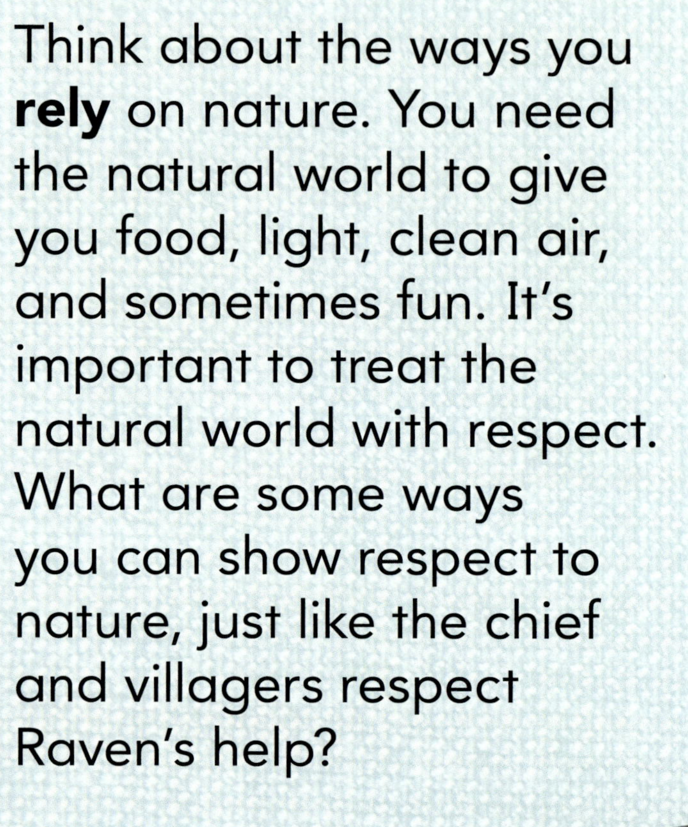

Think about the ways you **rely** on nature. You need the natural world to give you food, light, clean air, and sometimes fun. It's important to treat the natural world with respect. What are some ways you can show respect to nature, just like the chief and villagers respect Raven's help?

More Facts

- Many Indigenous peoples from the Northwest Coast of North America tell stories about Raven. These include the Haida, Tsimshian, and Tlingit peoples.
- Stories about Raven are known as Raven Tales.
- The Haida have a story about Raven finding the first people. They came from a large clam shell!
- Raven is a trickster. In some stories, he helps people. In others, he causes trouble!

Glossary

admit – to allow something to be true.

avoid – to stay away from something.

lesson – a teaching, or something learned.

rely – to count on.

traditional – describing something done regularly and over time by a group of people.

transform – to change shape.

Index

avoidance 9, 14

chief 6, 9–11, 19–20

fable 4

folktale 4–6, 14, 19

lesson 4, 14, 16–17, 19–20

nature 19–20

Northwest Coast 6

old man 9–11, 13–14

shape-shifting 6, 13

villagers 10, 19–20

Online Resources

To learn more about *Raven the Trickster*, please visit **abdobooklinks.com** or scan this QR code. These links are routinely monitored and updated to provide the most current information available.